ANASTACIA-RENEÉ

(v.)

Anastacia-Reneé

GRAMMA
POETRY

(V.) BY ANASTACIA-RENEÉ

COPYRIGHT © 2017

ALL RIGHTS RESERVED

PRINTED IN THE USA

ISBN 978-0-9987362-2-8

SECOND PRINTING

PUBLISHED BY GRAMMA POETRY

WWW.GRAMMA.PRESS

DISTRIBUTED BY SMALL PRESS DISTRIBUTION

WWW.SPDBOOKS.ORG

DESIGNED BY DREW SCOTT SWENHAUGEN

COVER ART :

APRIL 16, 1893 (POSITIVE PLATE SOLAR ECLIPSE, CHILE)

© 1997 LINDA CONNOR

INTERNAL VISUAL ART BY BOSTON SMITH

A - H
2

I - P
62

Q - Z
86

(v.)

a.

awe struck
asshole
as if
ashy
ash
as you were
at ease
attention
attentive
at ten you were too old to be 9
aint i a woman

b.

betrayal
behind
barstool
benevolent
becky
burn
babies breath
blues
been there
blind
benign

c.

cancer
coagulate
conjunction
cut (to the core)
collect
cull
cyst (systemic)
chorus

d.

death
decompose
deliver
divide
dream
dungeon
dear _____
don't know

e.

everything
encase
entity
envision
eight
ensemble
evolution
ear

f.

full
fuck
fog
fist
fear
famine
furnace
fallopian tube
fault (it is not yours)

g.

grit
gratitude
gone
gist
galvanized
gestation
gouhl
genesis

h.

hell
heliotrope
heaven
hymen
hill
hymn
hind
hell & heaven seem to start off the same. all
he & he until you have to figure out if you
want your purgatory to burn hot or cold & no
one ever really wants to choose until it's too
hot or too cold. he & he.

BECKY THE PATRON SAINT (WWBD)

you are trying to summon becky as   in   like

what would becky do (wwbd) in this situation would she be

sweaty palmed & red eye would she wonder if something as

simple as *this* (flat tire in the suburbs & expired tags) make her

call her kids & tell them she loves them (maybe for the last time)

make her pray to the moon for more light & less waning make

her wish a quick change of blue eyes & flippy blonde hair red

lips & a side of (my uncle went to the police academy (too)) so

you make her a patron saint. pray to becky for your safety. pray

when the cops come that becky mount you & speaks to the

officers in her tongue may she possess your face turn it anything

but black woman turn it pale or exotic tan on tuesday you say

becky please save me save me from the bony hands of my own

ancestors children save me from a simple traffic stop

3

GRIM [1]

the forest was a dusty shade of unforgettable & the girls, well,

the girls pretended as if they too were unforgettable their ankles

scuffing each other to keep warm & the leaves asking each

of them if they remembered (or not) & all of this thinking &

thinking & thinking made for a boring play & the audience

couldn't help but be ho hum & complacent & sonora decided

she'd liven up the dead play with a bit of purgatorial remarks

about forgetting & this well, this made the girls look smart even

when a thing began to deteriorate when it began attacking

itself when the setting began to look like child's play & improv.

& the girls, well, the girls told this story to themselves to keep

themselves awake in the woods & also to keep the wolf licking

their faces entertained because the wolf, well, the wolf was an

avid reader but lately had gotten really deep into theatrically

written work & the girls well, with the wolf licking them

decided they would give the wolf one hell of a forest story.

something unforgettable.

CURIOUS

CABINET OF NATURAL CURIOSITIES, ALBERTO SEBA

do you feel a wormless bird is a better bird than a bird with a (*worm*) in its mouth

you think that maybe having more heart is not a good thing you decide

no   no   no   it isn't

there is a page with an elephant, pig & human fetus you wonder which of those

is the most innocent which has shed the most blood the human one is sealed

inside something resembling a drive up glass sucky tube for money at the bank for

pens & withdraw slips & you wonder if anyone thought this embryo was priceless

if you are priceless if not if no way if nope   nope   nope what is your

     worth

                             dolla dolla

                             bills y'all

you wonder which is worse thinking you are priceless or thinking you aren't

     worth

(a) dime in the end you cannot survive by telling the world you are priceless

people want to know how much you charge you wish you could say you are not

     worth

any monetary amount   *bitches*   but the rent & water & car note

have to be paid curious things send you to places you never visit (like your dad's

grave) & you once watched a man with a santa clause beard take 3 puffs of a

loaned cigarette when all of the sudden at just the right time you looked & 2

maybe 3 teeth

fell from his bridge & you wondered *where is the blood*   in fact
you waited in your car to see the blood trickle to say to yourself *that was so*
            worth it

                    .

a curious unscripted scene that takes the pressure off you pondering whether or
not you value yourself (priceless) or $22.00 an hour

the precious corals are red & this makes you feel sick to your stomach makes you
think of sharks feasting on human fat & you can see (for yourself) on the page it's
coral   it's coral   it's coral (but)   you keep hearing *dadadadadadada*
jaws film score in your curious ears & you don't know why this coral (red) takes
you there to the time when you knew for sure   for sure jaws was in the guest
bedroom while you lay in the waterbed & the look on your face (priceless) when
you felt the waves underneath your bony ribs

b is a brush fooled butterfly it has 16 colors just on the wings alone & you are
curious about why its wings aren't larger then you think it probably wants to be a
goddamn bird & you are curious whether or not it would be able to hold a worm
inside its mouth & you think wouldn't that be (priceless) to see a butterfly
holding a worm & you might have more heart for it than you had for the bird &
you are curious if you took a picture what the price might be (focus)

(v.) you realize as you search the book for the most curious something you could ever be/not be curious about that you run across a serpent with 4 heads you are overcome with the feeling that you have seen this four headed serpent—that it once tried to attack your wife on your wedding day that your wife has tried repeatedly over & over again to remove the heads like nettles like wet sand from her ass   like bad noodles from a cambodian soup & you think you have named the third head a name you cannot utter but you know if you name it it will only rename (itself) it will only coil itself around itself & vomit the skin it's in & you are curious about digesting & vomiting how the smell of rope & defaced vaginas makes for any serpent's dream

CUT IT OUT PRICILLA

in the midwest winter the white girls frost their hair like farrah
faucet & nibble on graham crackers & strawberry flavored
lip gloss & this is way before lip gloss was poppin & can you
text me the address & you were just a little pookie when you
a–ha'd it *does* matter (your hair[1]) it *does* matter (your lips[2]) it
does matter (your skin[3]) & you memoir pricilla talking *at* you
during recess about her mom going to mexico to get a tan about
your complexion & you & long hair'd pricilla held your fuzzy
arms out/together & she said *not me i don't want to be as dark*
as you & you thought to yourself how the night sky is dark &
beautiful how chocolate cake makes all your classmates be quiet
& good how pricilla's mom said she wanted her own tall dark &
handsome man how pricilla told you she was lucky her daddy
was milked with more cream & you & pricilla were best friends
the whole 5th grade until she cut your free growing hair with
kid scissors until she called you a spic which didn't make sense
because you knew you were a nigger

1. your hair was the source of your mother's guilt, how she couldn't straight braid to save her life or cornrow anything but a drunk man's hair after lukewarm bourbon & salted peanuts. & you tried your best not to ever be tender headed when you bowed your head between her knees asking god to forgive you for 10-year-old sins. like the time she told you not to get your hair wet but you really, really, really wanted to put your sweaty body in front of that sprinkler because pricilla said your hair would dry long before the street lights came on, long before archie bunker or the jeffersons would come on tv, long before your mother would come home in her nurse's uniform & bleached hands & when your mother saw your freshly pressed uhura hair had suddenly turned all angela davis you thought of penny & the pressing comb scene on good times, you suddenly felt as if you deserved to be burnt toast or persecuted or grounded from your bike but she (your mother) grabbed the ice cream from the freezer & told you one day you'd have to learn the hard way about consequences of not doing what you're told, about being ungrateful, about what happens when a straight thing becomes wild.

2. pricilla said your lips were too big to ever put vaseline or lip gloss on them that they did a thing that looked like monkey lips & this is why you covered your mouth when you were spoken to why you hated your voice because it drew attention to your lips why you spent countless hours trying to shrink them with boiling water like your grandmother's greens on sundays.

3. your skin kept you on the outside: too light for dark girls too dark for light girls & you did not have a place (to be) all in one day you had been called stuck up all in one day you had been called blackie all in one day you had learned you were an outsider even on pricilla's side of the fence & she said she liked you *anyway* despite the way your legs looked in white shorts or your ankles in white sneakers or the way she asked you several times if you were sure you wanted to go out & play (in the sun). & you always told her it didn't matter to you if you got darker or not & once you told her the darker the berry the sweeter the juice & she told you that's fine but you're no berry & therefore you will never have sweet juice.

BLUES

when she hears

the blues

(zaffre) her body a horn

(baby) her body a piano

& those fingers run

themselves across

her black

when she hears

the blues

(sky) it's not always melancholy

(cobalt) not always tissue & mascara

sometimes it's just

(peacock) a draft in the summertime

(spruce) a cloud forming around the moon

her blues

(denim)not a crust of bread or

(azure)baby come back

her blues

(lapis) more like rainy day in a swim suit

(indigo)or too much jam

in a tight slippery space

AS TOLD BY MARY

I.

i want to hold a newborn in my arms
give her a name like trinity
i want to wear magenta eye shadow
& bake cookies for budding fifth grade   girls
but no one wants to utter   my name
for happiness' sake
not once or twice or even three times

bloody mary

2.

alice
my only confidant
spends her time telling me
about this pill
this hole
this rabbit
this head on
this head off
& who wants to keep changing
chanting into something
someone they're not/was/is   won't ever be

bloody mary

3.

when did it come to this
the summoners
bullied boys on nutrition breaks
wealthy sorority dare devils
soy candles in dark dorm rooms
lady fingers & eye lashes
saluting the air
13 times begging my face to appear
next to a toilet
sink/shower
not because i'm clean
but because they want to be

bloody mary

4.

it's not so easy to keep
blood behind the glass
the visitors twisting my ovaries
the world toying with   my worth

BACKPACK

I.

we wore our backpacks on our fronts because we thought it was innovative and cool. we know these words and others like **disenfranchised** or **propaganda**. but this isn't about big words, this is about a backpack. here ( ). this way we could be cool together and not worry about anything getting in the way of our arms this was before we were intimate and we were trying so hard not to rub our bodies against each other like crickets. backpacks on our fronts is the way we navigated the first couple of months. and one day, just like all the other days one of us unloaded our backpack and this became the longest recorded kiss between us. we call it the backpack kiss even though there was no backpack involved in the making of the kiss. and we couldn't stop kissing and this is why we are here ( ).

2.

the two of us didn't feel like being seen today not by anyone
who could cheerfully walk up to us and say hello. this time both
of us instead of one of us was in what we call a pitching bitch
mood. a pitching bitch mood is when one of us pitches a top
and just bitches about it for no reason and the other one of us
chooses to disagree, this then causes an extreme argument and
before you know it we are both pitching and bitching and we
don't know the reason for this symphony but we notice when
it happens because one of us says something like *we can stop this
pitching and bitching now*. the sun does this thing where it half way
shines on her and makes it seem like she's got three eyes instead
of two. i told her this in away that didn't sound too farfetched
or science fiction fantasy and she thought i was trying to say she
looked like an alien and this is not what i meant at all because
why would i call the person i loved an alien and because she
thought i was calling her an alien she called me a ghost and we
both know this is true and that is how we got here ( ).

(v.) when you danced on tuesday
you told her in your panties
that you didn't much uh huh
to lingerie but you would (if she asked)

when you put your lips against hers
you didn't hear any push away or pull (either)
but you inhaled/like jess from stone butch blues
in the middle of the alaska afternoon/snow bunny

when you put your finger in the middle of her nowhere
you pulled out nothing but change/how you offered her
your two cents(sense) in exchange for anything feeling worthy

& you have decided to make this a ritual:

1. make it warm in your room
2. wear a pair of sexy panties
3. tell yourself you'll fuck in the sun
4. imagine yourself worthy (of all the things)

AS TOLD BY A CHILD

"I AM NOT SORRY, I HAVE NOT SHED A TEAR FOR THE INNOCENT PEOPLE I KILLED. I WOULD LIKE TO MAKE IT CRYSTAL CLEAR I DO NOT REGRET WHAT I DID." Dylan Roof

I.

you used to think the number 9 was special
like if you saw it you would feel as though
you got the candy from the machine, the present
& getting to stay up later before bed
& when you are a child you think childish thoughts
& you feel safe & you think benediction
is like the soul train line only for jesus
& you want to go to church
not just cuz of candy in sunday school
but because you get to use your voice
as if it were an instrument for god
& you are young
& you think of this as if god is directing the choir
& you imagine yourself gods favorite singer
& you open your mouth
so wide you feel
as though
god can see your heart

2.

you hear that your number 9

is now a way to describe a merciless death

& you don't feel like you can

make a way out of no(way)

you understand what the grown folks mean (now)

by no ways tired but you are fatigued

& you call on your faith like you call your mama

when you want to know what's for dinner

& you don't hear any(thing) back this time

3.

you decide you will trust—you will lay your little hands

on your community

& make change

& that is the only thing

that makes sense when 9 people woke up

& prayed

& 9 people are now being prayed (for)

god bless the child that has his own

& you want your own answers

you want to ask dylan roof

if he ever sang in a church choir

if he ever sang so loud god could see his heart

DE(COLONIZE)

decolonize
colonize   i
colon

     release   toxins   waste
     lease   to   was   (has/not anymore)
     ease   in   as

co
no   (know/now)

appropriation
appropriate
a pro   (~~expert~~)

blackness
black
lack   (empty)

(v.)AN INCOMPLETE INVENTORY OF WHAT
YOU ARE MADE OF (:) *COLON*

1. brick
red bricks in all shapes
some chipped
some flawless
some only crumbs
some spliced perfectly/half patriarchy–
half parakeet

2. bones
some shaped like stars
some shaped like daggers
some smothered in dried blood
some with dirt
some babies fingers pointing out
some wishing

3. hair
straight
crooked
matted
fur'd
(   )
dead

4. lies
mother's
father's
mother's mother
father's father's
mother's mother's mother
father's father's father
mother's mother mother's mother
father's father father's father
slave masters
slave master's slave
trees
land
bible
heart
hades

land
bible
heart
hades

5. truths
mothers
fathers
mother's mother
father's fathers
mother's mother mothers
father's father's father
mother's mother mother's mother
father's father father's father
slave masters
slave master's slave
trees
land
(   )
heart
haiti

6. skulls
———
———
———
———
———

7. birds
ravens
butchered beaks
migrate migrate migrate
land
doves
nest eggs
cracked nest eggs
straw

8. ghosts: the haunting kind & the living kind
see through see through trans(parent)

(v.) questions: because hate is recycled, is the constitution compostable? what rhymes with institutionalization? if medication has the potential to brighten your urine, would it also be true that it could add gusto to your life? make you forget you are the color in the black and white? are there general casting call guidelines for historically stereotypical characters? is one deemed a triple threat if s/he can embody sambo, jezebel, chiquita banana or barbie? if "why are you so angry?" is a rhetorical question, does the answer sound proper & articulate?

AS TOLD BY LUNA

AFTER THE 2017 ELECTION

be a big gurl

roll your panties up fast

& your cunt squeezed in slow

stick your finger in your belly buttom

to make sure you are still breathing

take your light bulb & shake it the east

shake it to the west

shake it to the socket that loves you the best

be a big gurl

roll your panties up fast

& your cunt squeezed in slow

take your own pulse & beat

(your) heart until it stops keeping

time // be a witness // for the people

afraid to testify god is a woman

in a blue moo-moo

& praise

is what happens when coffee

is stirred

ANIMALS ARE THE CURE

my aunt is dying of cancer

my aunt is living with cancer

& i want to hold on to a frog

i want to smell

what a healthy frog is supposed to smell like

what does a frog smell like to other frogs

& does one frog say to another frog

you smell terrific today

it has to let me pet it

but not like a dog with hair

like a frog with no hair

like the same baldness that comes from chemo

it must croak in the palm of my helpless hands

my faith restored

the green breaths miraculous sounds

living/croaking/living/croaking/living

my aunt is dying of cancer

my aunt is living with cancer

& i want to see an opossum run over

not mashed to pieces or bloody

just unexpectedly run over

like the way you find out you have stage four

when nobody told you about stages one-three

why didn't i swerve

i want to watch the opossum's
foamy saliva creep down its lips
then to watch it rise from the dead & run
my hands covering my mouth
my faith   restored

(v.) confession #265
once i wore fuzzy pajama feet
& shared a steal of a deal house
with roaches & rats
all the rats being bullied by the roaches
all the humans being bullied by the rats
all the food just a hyphen
between survival & survival

_____ CAN HIDE SO BE VIGILANT. YOU HAVE _____ YAY! _____ BOO!

cancer— the thing you can survive if you can know it is coming. & you will not eat anything out of the can. no sir. you will only answer to fresh veggies & all things organic.

cyst— the thing that is systemic like racism or sexism or ageism or sizeism. & you will not become hysterical at the thought of removing anything that is not sustainable. no tryst with apathy   no-pus filled balloon of pretend.

fibrous— the thing that makes you regular. all those tiny fibers fibering & brosing. tiny little threads of us hanging out in the sacred nipple like *ommmmm*. the thing that never fibs either you are or are not bro not like bro where is my car more like   bro it's just us   bro   we could be a fraternity
fi bro ous   fi bro us   fi   bro   us

breast— the things we take for granted like rest   like water from the east
& we even get two kinda like   again. twice as nice.
                                                  two the hard way
apparently not as important as a leg or a thigh

nipple— the things you used to keep hope alive. to keep the baby birds open so that they could fly. & you have been told not to show them because only a real man farmer can show off his yams.   & you've been taught

squirting is a bad thing & showing it
even worse // starve your child until you get to a restroom
act as if it's been cut off (already)

(v.) fuck cancer

BIRDIE & THE BEAST/SPOTTED BIRD ATOP A TREE

& the bird cracked herself open & birthed a shell

& the shell split herself open & winged a beast

& the beast stood as tall as any beast who was not a beast (could stand)

& the standing beast who was tall enough to be a tall standing

      beast   bent   back

now the mysticism is not very mystical or perhaps its too mystical when you read the four lines & we see that the writer's (voice) isn't sure if the beast is really a beast or if it's just standing like a beast & we wonder if the writer knows that she's written about birds & shells—if she knows this might not be the thing to do if she wants to be published in a reputable magazine that maybe writing about birds, shells & beasts is not what they want & the writer will re-write it in a way that might seem more organized & formulaic so it is easily digested for the main audience (below)

the small white spotted bird was born of a translucent shell

                                      mother

the shell, miniscule but mighty gripped the bird as if the bird might fly

                                       womb

as if the bird might morph/transform herself into a beast

                                       blood

(v.) the metropolis is a place to eat your boneless young careful not to puncture a vein or wrap your death around plasma sell yourself to no one make yourself a tag less woman with two left breast tell the retail shop you can make a killing let them know you've got two sons each black each beautiful each with open flesh wounds boneless

DEAD TO YOU

the sisters tossed
their beads to the dead
like carefree & word to
your mother like we are
so accustomed to death
burial & resurrection like
come for me guédé
like we are ready to
take our place in the
death world like we
got our gowns ready
& waiting like let a
motherfucking cop
pull us over & shoot us
like we are ready to
leave this ole earth
like come & get us
whitie like we are
ready for you while
we do our lives while
we drive our children
to school in their
car seats while we
leave the store with
unleavened bread &

babies breath come for

us cop with your

uniforms & guns

we are already walking

dead we are already

ghostly bodies risen

& risen again & again

like you wanna see

a zonbi point your gun

at the temple of a black

woman who has already

been scorned & you will

have the privilege of fire

after fire after fire

you will get to see

a black woman wearing

a skeleton for a wedding

dress where she breaks

her bones for each vow

she takes

EIGHT DAYS LATE

if you are _____ & your period is eight days late you:

• imagine your period scared shitless staining a white room
folded up in a green chair. her face being slapped, her hands
bound while an interrogator says, *where were you on*
september 1st at 8 a.m.? did you or did you not say you
would be on time? do you have an alibi to support
your so called truth? this uterus you say you spent a
little too much time with…where is she now?

•• imagine your period awkwardly shopping for baby clothes. how she
wants to browse the girl's section but she knows. she knows for sure it
will be a boy. the lining always decorated in various shades of royal &
indigo. she traipses up to the counter suddenly realizing she needs eggs to
pay.

••• imagine her in stilettos & a micro mini. the choir singing the *men all*
pause. how the crowd gives her a last standing ovulation, the
audience weeping & shouting, job well done. her speech, long &
entertaining is interrupted by a note requiring at least ten more years of
work—the click clack of her leaving like a like a bloody sunset on the
first day of snow.

(v.) questions: does a length or proportion of time signify the end—as in you are now sexually mature? period. does a daisy asked to be picked? is a scar proof of a healing wound or evidence of profuse bleeding? is a carjacked hymen insured?

GRAPHIC NOVEL

I.

in the first picture there is a girl holding on to her dog & the
dog has fleas & the fleas feel sorry for the dog & the dog feels
sorry for the girl & the girl feels sorry for the mother who has
laid down with the dog who has the fleas & the fleas get inside
the girl & the girl is trying to talk to the fleas & the fleas do not
understand the word *no* & there is jumping

in the second picture the girl is wearing red rain boots & the
girl is smiling not because of the ice cream in her tiny finger
painting hands but because of the rain boots & the girl glares
at the red rain boots in a way that says can you see these fancy
rain boots & the man who purchased the rain boots is not a
man but a wolf & the girl does not know he is a wolf because
wolves don't buy rain boots & he did not lay in the bed & act
as grandma & at this point he is not aiming to take her bread
basket & there is joy (there *is* joy) about rain boots & the happy
girl with the ice cream & rain boots is talking to her rain boots
& she is telling them they are the best & the man behind the
camera is asking her how much she likes her rain boots & she is
saying she likes them so much & he licks his lips & her so much
& he tells her he will buy her a pair of blue ones next time &
the girl in the second picture decides she would be very happy
with blue rain boots & she waits & in the picture she asks the
man behind the camera when will he buy her the boots & he
says after this picture but first eat your ice cream & she does &
this girl is the happiest she thinks she's been

3.

in the third picture the girl's hair is pressed & bouncy & she
is looking very 70's cutie pie & she smells like baby powder
& baby oil & her knees are shiny & her elbows too & she has
Vaseline on her lips. & she fidgits in the picture because her butt
crack is itchy & she tries to tell her mother about this itchy butt
crack & too tight blue boots but she does not know how to
speak her mothers language she does not know how to throw
up a red flag & she decides maybe ice cream will make her itchy
butt crack better that if she takes off her socks blue boots will fit
better & this is how she learns to survive

ESSAY TEST QUESTIONS

A.   A COP KILLS YOUR SON

B.   YOU SON KILLS HIMSELF

C.   A COP TRIES TO KILL YOUR SON

D.   YOUR SON TRIES TO KILL HIMSELF

E.   HIS MOTHER DIES FROM THE POSSIBILITIES

(v.) for parenting:
    there is no manual
    there is no manual
    there is no manual

GOOD IS NOT ENOUGH

there is an academic in my pocket   her locs in a bun

when i i tell her it's her turn   she reminds me of _____

she tells me when you get

right down to it   all the _____ in the world means_____

i feed her twice a day

a fat meal of

alphabet fat & credentials

a silver spoon of better & way

(v.) confession #259
i'm the creepy girl in all the scary movies
who can read minds & has visions.
all the people shouting from the
70's couches *carrie, carrie, carrie.*

CARNIVAL

I.

your belly a carnival for passersby step right up flop when
the travelers pause beckon them jelly rolls & cannibals open
mouth ahhhhh spinning top show them dizzy in a little town
face painted with disappointment & hysteria get your peanuts
crack crack shell freak cadaver weeeeeeeeeeee kettle corn
cage amniotic fluid neverland tiny tubes you have never had
your insides palmed like this belly a straw for drunken sailors
celebrate fundus! fundus! fundus! ovation honorable behavior
& pear-shaped girls discount rentals baby i will marry you your
belly a receptacle for too sticky/too sweet cotton candy &
mountainous shades of red red red flush neon flicker blue blue
blue for your belly button up a home for nostalgia & maggoty
road maps which way is up inside the belly carnival & tallest
ferris wheel in a blink town called no body & what cannibal
wants to be inside no (body) sell yourself get at least one hot dog
sold to the biggest biter see who will ride & die rosy belly ring
around & stop cadaver stretch all your tracks all aboard lines lines
lines trains coming through never staying stand in line say this
carnival is ohhhh ahhhh lights lights lights & babies get in free

tonight mwah! your lips blood red, your eyes white, your ribs
blue say you resident, civilian, call you mammy, jezebel, call you
anything but upper crust of bread. today you will be cornbread
you will be sopped in whatever there is—it's all gravy baby bet
mary nan peg sary slave self resurrect dance dance dance dance
nigga dance dance dance nigga show the cannibals what you are
working with outside you cannot remember the smell of your
own discontent dollars ray charles saying something (

)whirl whirl whirl
weeeeeeeeeeeeeeeeeeeeeeeeeeeeeeeeeee lights lights lights & you
know that this is not a scripted kinda thing like housewives or
bad girls this is real real real pink pink pink all in your god blue
blue blue ribs is what they eat & you want to tell them shed stop
picking, stop adding extra sauce stop licking fingers stop licking
your torso up & down & up & down weeeeeeeeeeee his again
again again mommy again again see that b(lack) girl don't you
grow up to be like her see that black girl don't you ever bring
her home if you fuck her fuck her in the city in the back
of a red mazda on the corner of ___ past & present progress
does not mean give her your last name you hear me weeeeeeee
again again again mommy stop licking shoving my bones inside
your pants boner grace eat at least one hot dog ride & die rosy
ring around your neck ray charles saying something georgia be
my georgia tonight let me kiss you until your blue shows on the
outside you cannot remember the smell of your own discontent

dollars dollars weeeeeeeeeeeeeeeeeeeeeeeeeeeeeeeeeeeeeeeeeeeee on
thee in the back of a red mazda i can't stand—my torso again
mommy again you hear me resurrect

DEAR LITTLE GIRL,

you must fight.

someone will hurt you.   hold you down.

someone will hurt you inside.   break thighs.

someone will hurt you inside: bone. vessel. cell.   enter in the exit.

you must wake up & fight.

parts of you will be stolen.   your hymen

parts of you will be stolen inside.   in the lost & found

parts of you will be stolen outside.   bone. vessel. cell.

you must wake up & fight. now.

remember you are not a little girl.

remember you are not a little girl but   god .

                    amen.

            a lower case *n* make such a remarkable difference:
            violet— a herbaceous plant of temperate
            regions, typically having purple, blue or
            white five-petaled flowers one of which
            forms a landing pad for insects.

            violent— using or involving physical force
            intended to hurt, damage or kill someone
            or something.

            ****

            VIOLET VIOLENT VIOLA VIOLATE

(v.) confession # 254
once there were 16 showers

IT'S NOT THAT I THINK
YOU ARE GOING TO HELL IT'S
JUST THAT I DON'T THINK
YOU ARE GOING TO HEAVEN

you have final answered you won't hide it anymore

won't hide the bone that tumbles out of your mouth

when you say vodun (voudou)/when they say hoodoo (boo-boo-boo)

when you say louisiana creole & they say southern gals

when you say altar & sacrifice & they say communion & bread

when you say dressed in white & they say dressed in white

there have also been several murders of vodou priests/priestesses, most recently

after the earthquake. christians were also said to have been keeping food aid for

themselves and stopping it from reaching vodou communities. in haiti, some

christians consider vodou a form of devil worship

you have decided since

you've been called a witch (anyway) you will

not run from the   dust in your eyes

you will not be sniff-sniff-sniff

that your powers are misunderstood

won't wear a turtle neck when vampires seek you out

in the light if they fang you with gimmie this

& gimmie then stain you with their

you should give me more (disappointment)

you have cowerie shell decided yes,

you have put a spell on you & that's okay

there have also been several murders of vodou priests/priestesses, most recently

after the earthquake. christians were also said to have been keeping food aid for

themselves and stopping it from reaching vodou communities. in haiti,

some christians consider vodou a form of devil worship

that you are the holder

of many brooms & your mojo exists in mason jars

that you do howl at the moon &

drowned your demons (face first) in the ocean

watched them choke on their own

sins & you are tired-tired-tired of apologizing

for it, tired of saying i'm sorry when you have

a waking vision or dream tired of keeping it

inside when you see dead people, dead animals

or dead love. you have decided you will not hide

anymore from your destiny that you are too tired

to keep running from (it) at this pace that your heels

have grown callous that your get up & go

has got up & gone into the cauldron &

there have also been several murders of vodou priests/priestesses, most recently

after the earthquake. christians were also said to have been keeping food aid for

themselves and stopping it from reaching vodou communities. in haiti,

some christians consider vodou a form of devil worship

you are not a-scared of ravens or crows or

vultures or black cats that cross your path

because if you are already a spirit & not of

this world you are not afraid of spirits or

things that are not of this world. & you don't

worry when there are times there is unexplained

light in your pictures or writing that is not

your (own) you are too tired to keep up this

protection of yourself

there have also been several murders of vodou priests/priestesses, most recently

after the earthquake. christians were also said to have been keeping food aid for

themselves and stopping it from reaching vodou communities. in haiti,

some christians consider vodou a form of devil worship

& you are too tired of telling

stories that make sense to mortal man to cover up

the spiritual things (happen)ing. & you are tired

of being tired & telling your selves that they can

come out one day. & some might say if you are

that psychic why didn't you know _____

_____ why

didn't you do _____

& you want to ask them if they are a human why did

they get a cold? why did they eat unhealthy food?

& you want to tell them even a spirit has to live

her life (on earth) even a spirit (on earth) is hardheaded

even a spirit (on earth) hangs her head down (lo)

even a spirit shoves herself inside a box

& packs herself away neatly until it's time

HEMOGLOBIN [CELL]

a red blood cell
having no hemoglobin

is called a ghost

you ride yourself
so that you cannot
be seen

a red blood cell
having no hemoglobin

is called a ghost

you boo inside your
heart so as not to
haunt any(one) else
it's just not fair to
leave them shaking
there as the dark
leave them all
i can't see you
there as the fear
leave them wondering
if in fact they ever
existed

a red blood cell
having no hemoglobin

is called a ghost

& you side to side as if you
are the side as if you are
other side of the side. stuff
your zombie in the seat of
your tomorrow so as not to
keep your present from being
unwrapped

DIGITS

1:11
prayer:
dear god
you can do anything.
idk why
stop the pain. like instantly.
praying
making it sound like shazam.
make know it's gone.
show me listening
fall out of the sky like
unexpected bird poop—
proof of shit happening.

2:22
meditation:
_____in
_____out
all is well.
i am well.
i am grateful.
20 seconds left..
use me as a vehicle for change.
use me as a vehicle to ...

3:33
wish:
i wish i was not
a girl. i wish i
didn't have to ride
this bus. this late
this time. this day
this man.
this finger
this skin
this grunt
this wet
not a girl
late bus man.

1:11
prayer:
merciful allah.
you can do anything.

end this war.

bring my son back to life.
change stained blood
to cherry stains. show me lightening.
fall out the sky like
unexpected silence—
proof that peace is happening

2:22
meditation:
breathe.
breathe.
i am removing ego.
life is not about me.
i need nothing.
i am nothing. just as everything
is & everthing. there is balance.
enlightenment is near...

3:33
wish:
this bith would
stop talkin' crazy
about her fuckin'
fries being cold when i
got them muthafuckas
straight out the vat
... she was would stop pointing
in my face with those
30 dollar french manicured
hands. & she got the nerve
to get a diet coke with a
big mac and apple pie.

1:11
prayer:
god ur not
        real.
        i'm

wtf? smh
@myself.

2:22
meditation:
om

_____

nothing.

3:33
wish:
1.
2.
3.
4.
5.
6.
7. & that
daddy could
live with us
again.

DRAGON

one of *them*. **anisozygoptera** never use your six legs. never run
when you should never hop **anisozygoptera** never jump ship.
let yourself be all forward, backward & side to side time you
use more dragon & less fly. who needs legs anyway when the
predators aim straight for the knees. cut you down when you
are begging to be raised. tell you your bony legs aint shit/aren't
worthy/not even defecation. **anisozygoptera** that whether
you got one, two, three four, five or six years experience/legs/
lifetimes/dead babies that you are only as valuable as the next
ones pointed resurrection.

EYES ARE ON IT

dear sparrow

how you flew
      then landed

we
      watched you

un-fly yourself
      upward to the moonlight

christen your feet
      within a wrecked nest

black sparrow
      raise your dead

tell your bones
      on this night

how you flew
      then landed

dear sparrow

(v.) confession # 266
i have counted them

all the little girls
first missing
last dead
& to some it's cnn.com headlines.
my heart vomits
all the chunky pieces of rage
splattered.
the thought of their bodies
now ghosts in the morgue.

FAT MEAT AIN'T PLEASING

it's as if we aren't allowed to dance with our clothes off
do not show the broken shatter of a fat stretch mark
beneath a skinny line of faith do not be brave
& look see about jiggling imperfections
in ridges of skin rosary. no magazine wants to parade
your holiness down the cookie cutter pews
it's as if your speckled back is a lonely devil fighting
to sin up the town

(v.) 157 stretch marks.

GRIMOIRE

FELICIA FELIX-MENTOR'S OCCASIONAL OUTBURSTS OF LAUGHTER WERE DEVOID OF EMOTION, AND VERY FREQUENTLY SHE SPOKE OF HERSELF IN EITHER THE FIRST OR THE THIRD PERSON WITHOUT ANY SENSE OF DISCRIMINATION. SHE HAD LOST ALL SENSE OF TIME AND WAS QUITE INDIFFERENT TO THE WORLD OF THINGS AROUND HER.

I.

how can
laughter be devoid of emotion
does the face not bend
the belly not suspend comedy
between abdomen & diaphragm
am i not three in one
how can you say my soul is lost
when i know
exactly where i left it last.

2.

zonbi: haitian

nzumbe: animated corpse

zora neal hurston

said i was a—fabricated felicia.

medical marvel not *zonbi*.

zora said, *not a real instance of death & resurrection.*

                                          made her promise

erzulie d' en tort

resurrect

each sullied fingertip.

hold tight to the waist of earth.

swathe volcano's.

thwack southern clouds.

resurrect

two beet lips.

utter light in stagnant water.

blow my breath on every shell.

collect them for your altar.

resurrect

one eye. then two.

substitute bla<u>n</u>k for blac<u>k</u>.

black for red.

red for gold.

3.

dear zora
my soul gathered up
a river. a blues. a mule.
down to joplin

visitation
the place where the living
kneel next to hollow bones
pitty. they forgot
or do not know
you've risen.

meet me old friend
all saints' day
meet me in a gingerbread house
bring felicia—miss her
black eyes & hymn
trudging feet & laughter
sing zora
while you wait.
I will bring
clove scented cookies & louise
have her scribe our vision again.

4.

2005. she swallowed us whole
back to herself. back to her insides
back to her heart. how many i do not know.
we stayed quiet. she held us. for a time.
            then let us go.
when we walk through the earth
call us paranormal. call us demons.
call us zombies. but we think—
in your unconscious state you
would rather be risen from the
dead than living below
the light you've been called to be.

5.

eolithic kith. blood, skin, roots & kin

i (felicia felix-mentor) stand beside you

i mourn as you leave for work

the weight of the world forcing your shirts inside your pants

i want to touch palms

feel the prophesies shift from m to n

i am _____

you see me _____

the corners of your eyes are not blank

the corners of your eyes are not black

i am full of energy & anxiety

i know—you have it too

hypertension

let us both denounce salt from

the rooms in our bodies

lest it banish us all (back) to

our graves.

GRIM (2)

when goldilocks arrived in _____ she realized she left her

favorite gloves in _____ how she sobbed for a grinder she could

feel slide down the back of her sooty throat & though she fit

right in sipping freshly ground organic coffee from the café with

the hardback books one everyone's to-read list she couldn't help

but wonder what the three bears were talking about two tables

down from her how she wanted to join in but not like she had

before not to colonize or appropriate anyone's *stuff* more like just

piano her clammy fingers down one of the bears chest & tell the

other that chair he was sitting in was too hard that he needed

something soft to lay his head down upon that she was the best

goldilocked granola in all the land.

DEAR MARY,

your lamb is not so little
your lamb is not so white
she's bloody, mary
& three times the sinner
she hoped to be
can you be sure to go
take her to a place
where she finds rest
where her matted hair
won't weaken & her
reflection won't
steal a single soul

i.

insipid
ill-na-na
interior
idle
irreplaceable
ick

j.

jim crow
jewel
juxtaposition
jinx
jellyfish
judy
j-walk
jam as in this patriarchy is not the jam

k.

knife
knit
kind
kept
kill da _____

l.

leviticus
loath
lisp
love
learned behavior
lusty
lend
lunge

m.

man (the)
monster (the)
mole
moon (the)
mangled
masturbation
mini
mono

microscopic
micro (aggressions)
mea culpa
mercy
merci
mother may i
mutilated (clit)

n.

no
no
no
no
no

o.

orphan
orchid
obtuse
orgasm
on & on
oh
orisha
omnipotent
om
orpheus
ode (to dead black men)
ode (to dead black women)
ode (to dead black children)
ode (to black president)
ode (to the you that was the you
that is no more)

p.

purple-tyranian, imperial, mountain majesty
plum, amethyst
pine
philanderer
para
paranormal
pedophile
poach
poach
period (first day)
please
predatory

preamble
purgatory
pussy
persona
part time
panic
paraphrase
pigeon

I JUST LOVE HER SO MUCH

the women inhale coffee while lulu lemon sweaters dangle like
static in hair or flaccid dicks or participles while they dote & coo
over michelle obama & they must have said classy & strong &
strong & classy & humble & smart & classy & strong & graceful
& witty & intelligent & classy & strong (not feminist) a million
times (sitting next to you) & there you are & they never even say
good morning (hi, hello, go to hell) never even think of you that
way never even care to notice // talk about michelle as if they
are on a first name basis with her as if she is coming over to go
shopping or talk about how to raise black girls in white america
& what it might be like if she & her husband walked down a
regular street in hoodies & sneaks // never even look your way
once (hi, hello, go to hell) & you think maybe you are not strong
or classy or lulu lemon enough for these women maybe you
are just an everyday nigger & you are not angry or jealous of
michele obama or oprah winfrey you have just come to realize
you are not the kind of woman of color who will hang on any
white person's wall (with thumbtacks)

PREDECESSORS

JANET DAMITA JO JACKSON

you remember hearing janet jackson's, nasty & thinking that's the kind of girl
you wanted to be all nasty, nasty boys, don't mean a thing. & that janet said the
only nasty thing she liked was a nasty groove & you weren't so sure what all that
involved but janet had control. janet told those nasty boys what to do.

<blockquote>
i'm not

a   fool

i

just

want

some

respect
</blockquote>

& that song made you confused because she was saying no to the nasty & yet yes
to the nasty (on her terms) & this is where you first learned that sex & power
don't have anything to do with love. & you told _____ that he was a nasty
boy. & you imagined he would bow down like those boys in the video (but he
didn't) & he asked you if you wanted to see how nasty he was & you crooned
out an ambivalent yes because this worked for janet jackson & you wore a black
shoulder-padded jacket & your hair was almost, almost as long and wavy as hers
(because your mother would not let you cut it or perm it). & you realized the
boys seemed to like when she was mean. the boys seemed to like when she was
not interested. the boys seemed to like when she rounded her lip at an angle just
beneath the left side of her nose & because you liked _____ so much you

told _____ he was a nasty (midwest–southern accent) boy & he better be
a gentleman or he'll turn you off & to stop! just like that & you put your piano
fingers up just like janet jackson & he did (stop). & he looked at you like you stole
something because his friends were around & you did (steal something) & he gold
tooth smirked at his friends & gold tooth smirked at you & harked & spat you a
silly little stupid skinny bitch (in your grade it was popular to preface everything
with the word little) & turned real nasty & he said something like you must be
crazy to think i would bow down to you & he said you like it was in slow-motion
& a foreign language & all your friends felt sad for you & you wanted to know
why they didn't join you like janet jackson's friends why they didn't rise up in
their outfits & dance like the boys were easy to forget why they didn't say stop
& you wondered if this would have gone better if you looked differently you
wondered how long people at your school would talk about this nasty repeat gone
bad[1]

---

1. & that next week after school _____ tried to walk you home & said you looked cute in your
print jeans & matching headband & all of the sudden he smelled like comet to you, like. all you
wanted to do was use him to clean the ring around your reputation.

jamesetta hawkins (jaamesetta hawkinz)
everyone is all sniffle & nose blow
that you're *at last*
is now nostalgia (think about this on sundays)

where were they
when your dizzying neon light
was earthbound

was she etta james or etta jones // isn't that beyoncé s song?

couldn't hum any other song you sang
couldn't tell you (born january 25th 1938) anything about you
heard of you from beyoncé
faint memory of an old folks conversation
over bones, beer & bbq

& me i knew you
see you & nina & ella & billie & sara & dinah & carmen & lena & betty &
_____ & _____ & _____ &_____ & _____ & _____
trading lipsticks & agony
your voices blaring on the overhead speaker
all the angels misty eyed/smoking/bobbing their heads

NOT MY PRESIDENT

you were graham cracker 8

when he was your mr. president

& your father was away at war & you were

the only brown family on the military base

whose mother was crying on her ashy knees

saying thank you thank you a black president

& you & your brother decided to yell

yay mr. president yay mr. president &

your mother said don't you'll get us killed

& you wonder why this was true until

a new president elect reminds you of the

men who were your neighbors of the men

who made you & your brother shh shh shh

of the men who sulked the very next day

saying this is the end of the united states

as we know it & you wanted to be somewhere

in america where there was rejoicing

somewhere in america where you could

touch your hand against the screen &

say *look mama look* & you remember 8

years ago having to fake-say

not my president not my president

when you shopped at the commissary

so you have lots of practice for today

PIGEON [BABY]

I.

it is a thing to think about:
the pigeons where are the
babies

2.

it turns out pigeons stay in the
nest for 40 sometimes 80 days
as in they come out when they
are practically adults

3.

your baby pigeon is out in the world
& there he is walking & searching
for bread & you don't like all the
men sprinkling his sidewalk
& you want to tell him only eat
the best crackers

4.

you tell your baby pigeon who looks like
a grown up pigeon in disguise that
he is in his jesus years (a bit early) that
he is a prophet (like marvin gaye) that
he has to stop walking & fly & he says
his wings are too heavy that no one
can see how special he is when he's with
the other pigeons

5.

when you take him home to revisit his nesting
he tells you he longs for the days of nest
by the water of cliffs so high no one could
see him of being called (respectfully) rock dove

6.

hide your babies
hide your babies
hide your babies

SO THE SCIENCE TEACHER TELLS THE GIRLS, "YOU KNOW, YOUR PARENTS REALLY SHOULD PACK YOU HEALTHIER LUNCHES & I KNOW THIS IS A COMMON THING WHERE YOU LIVE BUT IT'S JUST ANOTHER THING THAT SLOWLY KILLS YOUR PEOPLE. HAVE YOU EVER HEARD OF YOGURT OR VEGGIE STICKS?"

the twin b*lack* girls

all braids & puffs

eat hot cheetos

        like manna   like desire

& one b*lack* queen

says she only likes

her cheetos hot

because heat

is a thing

she can feel

because this
kind of stigma
she can see   like evidence   of a crime
                     like a promise   of a begged thing
hot cheetos
& the words
cascade from
her lips   like waterfall   like holy

nobody wants
to see a black girl
flying
everybody wants
to see a black girl
fall to the ground
on her face   like evidence   of a crime

LOOK WHAT I FOUND

you unearth yourself like a fossil
you cannot answer when they say
what are these

& you wonder about the shape you are in
all your genetics whirl pool & cuneiform
you don't want to use a pick or a rake
or hear them say
use the hoe
you know you don't want your pieces
                              excavated

no

there are people using 8 dollar words to talk about race &
race relations & you think that's great

all that you can hold in your mouth today is this:

no

& you know it isn't frosting on a gluten free cupcake or
phd-esque but it all you can muster with the vulnerability
of the self spread around like hummus on a whole foods cracker

no

the women are wearing pricey clothing & expensive jewelry & they are
slaying it with the power in their education & the white people are
nodding their heads like yes you are speaking in the perfect language
so that I can be your ally but all you can push out of your barren lips is

no

& this will not put you in the best publications or land you a book on the
best seller list or get you cirucluated as an educated black woman on
the scene but—your lineage is a worker bee's haven for desiccated wombs
& deaf ventricles (swarm) & all you can revolution up is

no

OH!

dress yourself up
a four legged
animation make
them laugh or
wince oh hologram
build yourself as a
dictionary for words
gone wrong paint
all the pages fuck
you & say sorry
(or else) turn the
pages furiously
like a fever eclipsing
a blistered dialogue
what happens when
you pop // dysfunctional
close walk your bits
back to dropping on
the kitchen floor see
how you are easily
swiffered & shoved &
jived tighten your neck
as a turkey gobble your
own epidermis oh twin
spirit of yourself build you

a tunnel to vision anything

neon or never or nothing

or narrow or not right now

or nauseous or nerve wracking

or neophyte notice how you never

show your teeth when you cry

never whip out your nails

when you are pointing

& this is your life's holy grail

a sunset too bright for your

heart a moon too low for your spirit

oh mirror look away

from what you know

is there drag your four legs

& crawl to the edge of (dis)grace

ON FACT AND FICTION

dear beloved, i used to think you were just hairball & hysteria

i used to try & understand how a woman gets dissected from

her soul. how her soul becomes a headless horseman roaming

her womb. i used to wonder why a woman would circle her

discontent as if it were a ka'bah. & no woman wants to put

shea butter on stretched out nostalgia. once the mark is there,

prevention is futile. i used to think this blue background on a

yellow day was fiction. that growl & cry was a morrison thing. &

now i want to tell dear toni that she sure knows how to capture

hideously beautiful things. like _____ & of course _____

too.

(v.) in these dreams you are always the second to be spoken to. you are always given left overs
& could-have-beens. you dream other dreams still of desmond tutu asking you for a reading from
his grave & you mustering up something which is similar to a prayer after famine. you wake from
this dream wanting still all your alone shoved down your throat with doritos & chocolate covered
umbilical cords & you cannot figure out which reality it is you are dreaming. better to stay awake
your wings fluttering flick flick flick your hands saying take good care.

PSALMS FROM A 16-YEAR-OLD'S LIFE BIBLE

PSALM 77

you could go to school & get shot at lunch while eating a dry peanut butter & jelly sandwich your mother made you with a note that says i love you. it could be your best friend's dad's gun. he could be mad at you because you _____ or anything. blessed are the boys who eat lunch

PSALM 62

you could be walking to the library really slow because you are tired from the day getting your english literature mandatory reading & get stopped by the police. they could rip your hoodie off & spit on your genes. you could live. you could die. *es no importa* (your spanish teacher just said that to you & you really liked the sound of it) blessed are the boys who walk to the library.

PSALM 23

you could be driving your mother's car to the grocery store to get flour for the chicken you want & get shot. because you _____ or anything. you could tell them you need to grab your wallet which is under the seat because it fell. because you are a new driver & didn't think to put it in the glove compartment. you might try to tell them you need to grab it. you might try. you. might. try. *es no importa.* _____ or anything. blessed are the boys who search for wallets.

PSALM 47

you might get asked by three jocks all at once why you aren't going to homecoming. they might say is it because you can't find a boy? they might have a moment of compassion, might say maybe you are not gay—try, just try to take a girl & see what happens. you might hear all your friends talk about suits & shoes & corsages & hair spray. you might sit in your room in the dark eating a peanut butter & jelly sandwich your mother made with a note that says i love you. blessed are the gay boys sitting in the dark.

PSALM 56

you might have a craving to hang out with a guy over 30 who knows some stuff. you might try not to miss your dad who is over 30 & knows some stuff. knows you. you might say fuck him in your journal _____ or anything. you might look in the mirror & wonder why you have the same face. you might feel the depression about this making you sick. you might throw up & not clean your bathroom properly. *es no importa.* (you remember your spanish teacher being thrilled you liked this phrase) *es no importa.* you might try & clean the bathroom. well. your teacher might tell your mother you are not living up to your full potential. you think to yourself you might get shot at lunch anyway. blessed are the boys whose fathers are disappointing.

(v.) hello, is there anyone on the mainline? i'm calling because//& i tried yesterday when/& they said to call him up & tell him what i wanted//hello?

we're sorry the mainline has been disconnected or is no longer in service. if you feel you have reached the mainline in error, please check the number & try again

(v.) hashtag real world problems
hashtag how did we get (here)
hashtag 22 degrees/homeless people/need blankets
hashtag dead babies in the trashcan
hashtag molestation molestation molestation
hashtag oppression/pressure/prisoner/
hashtag internalized racism
hashtag really/yea/right now/2017
like   like   like like like   like   like   like   like   like   like

MASTER TALE

we hid our accents (act/sense) never wanting our masters to know (no) who we really were. we dressed (the part) & made/maid our hair as perfect as perfect could be. when it was time to separate us, first by color, then by body type, we tried very hard to appear stone-faced and complacent, always texting each other & emailing our disapproval in code. i guess i should feel lucky—my master plans on giving me a 401(k) and time off after i have my child. he laughed and said, *can't wait to have that one on board with the company too!*

in the field we always have to watch our bent backs to make sure no one is going to undo all that we've done (no unkempt braids/we want to loc). we always have to hold each other up without anyone knowing we might topple over   we might get fatigued (camouflage)   we might for(get) to make sure the cotton is picked just right & when we go on our smoke breaks/brakes & shuffle to Starbucks we always make sure we get back/black before our white colleagues we always make sure we are early to work & pay extra for parking because of it we always make sure we don't eat chicken at lunch time so as not to come back with greasy lips or slippery hands because no one wants the master to say *had chicken for lunch eh?*
& we try our best to hold each other up   we try our best to cover for each other when one of us is down down down way deep in the fields when one of us has lost all shuck & jive & accidentally returns from lunch late with a feather or two & a bit of blood soaked through our cotton shirts.

"...KILL US."

you know this is not the alpha or omega

of this statement that this here kingdom come

(came) down that a small voice expressing

fear & "us" is as long time ago & fractured

as racism that some little boy years & years ago

said, "they're trying to kill us" mama & they did   (kill)

& you are not sure how to process a baby

wrapped in mama's arms & her being shot & it

being all over the news & people are keeping tabs

about what she did wrong about her sanity

                    crazy black bitch

about if she had a right to be angry or to have

weapons if she had a right to be a human

if she was human if her baby was a baby or

a monkey on her back & you know "they're

trying to kill us" is trapped at the bottom of all

oceans is overboard & above & in between

time & you feel like (keeping tabs) it could be true for

you & yours too, "they're trying to kill us."

"they're trying to kill us." "they're trying to kill us."

(v.) the officers will be placed on administrative leave, which is standard procedure in officer-involved shootings, according to police.

JUDY

call me   judy

pretend my mother is becky my father ryan

pretend everything i say is the truth—just because.

pretend i wrote it

pretend i am intelligent & creative

pretend i work hard—for the money

                              donna summers on your dick

                    if you need it.

call me   judy

pretend i am the white fence

pretend i am the big house

pretend i am the dog. make it a lab. make it golden.

pretend i drink cosmos. smoothies after a workout.

pretend i smell like—prell

                              lips like bonnie bell

                              victoria secrete model

                    if you need it.

call me judy

pretend i dominate history

pretend i am the love

pretend i take little things (culture)

pretend i am exotic.

pretend i have soul—like a black woman.

        jill scott/tracy chapman/nina simone   *goddamn*

        afro wig & wide lips/hips

        if you need it.

N

I

O

q.

quiet
question
quench
quantum
queer
quiver
quadrillion
quotient

r.

railroad
right hand
rusty nail
rent
real talk
resist
robbery (appropriation)
road block
really though
revelation
rinse
roll-up (on you)
regal
raw
rearview mirror (hindsight)
ready (or not)
risky

s.

social awkwardness
sex in the bathroom
social media sickness
soy
semi
serial killer
serial killer
serial killer
stop
sun/son
seize
synchronicity
sinner (s)
succubus
sorrow
selah

sordid
settle
sweat
soil
saffron
sinking
sing
soon come
salve
shelter
sheep
salpinx
sarcotic
sup)

t.

two lips
tone
term II
tony for short
time machine
tear up
turn up
team up
turmoil
tree (mama)
toothless
tough
today
to be continued
to be honest
to be fair
temerity
transience
turtle
temporal
tulip
tropophobia

u.

under
unwind
unwanted
unconditional
uprising
uterus
uplift

up rise
utter
until
unjust
unsatisfactory
unison
uh (no)
up jump the boogie
unicorn

v.

verb
ventricle
vagina/vagina/vagina
vertigo

vine
vision
vast
vehement
variety
voice
vagina/vagina/vagina
violent
violate
violet
village
void
vortex
vow
vampire
valid
vagina/vagina/vagina
vessel
v.i.p.
vanish

w.

water
war torn
ward off
worm
wayward
wish
way-make-er
why
word(werd)
whoa
wick-wick-wack

witch
wound
worthy
womb
whiteness
worship
worn
wow
wrapped
wam
whole story (as in the truth)
wind
wrong way

x.

x-ray
xenophobia
xanthocomic
xenomorph
xeric

x.y.z.
x. (as in place an x marking how you identify so we can put you in a box)

y.

yes
yoni
yarn
youth
ya heard
yoke
yoga
yourself
yonder
yell

z.

zilch
zombie
zonbi
zealot
zoom
zinnia

WHAT'S YOUR EMERGENCY

one cop to another:

we are out of chalk

murder	pop	cop	murder	pop	cop
murderer	pop	cop	murderer	pop	cop
murder	pop	cop	murder	pop	cop
murderer	pop	cop	murderer	pop	cop
murder	pop	cop	murder	pop	cop
murderer	pop	cop	murderer	pop	cop
murder	pop	cop	murder	pop	cop
murderer	pop	cop	murderer	pop	cop
murder	pop	cop	murder	pop	cop
murderer	pop	cop	murderer	pop	cop

ZOMBIE (1)

you will never tell them you are a zombie
that you have been awake since the last
time you were killed that your   metamorphosis

is a lucid nightmare sticky with hope & antifreeze
that you have schooled yourself to walk with your
hands down to your side/drop your   shoulders

that you have learned not to do the sambo shuffle
let your legs drive your feet (instead) & the dogs
try & sniff you out try to make you   remember

who you were when you were a(live) make you recognize
your silhouette when it can't feel the sun or raindrop
whispering down the calamity in your   jane

RISKY SIDE
(IN ALL LANGUAGES)

you have been told you have to go to the at risk side of the clinic

you are young & you do not understand at risk which is to say

you didn't know about the risks you were taking which is to say

you didn't k(no)w there could be an un-risk time (in your situation) &

on your way to the at risk clinic you saw your beautician & her

son & you remember people telling you do not let her do your hair

she has hiv & when you saw here being held up by her son how she

looked radiant & glamorous & angelic even & she said to you get tested

& if you don't have hiv live your life like a motherfucker

& if you do have h.i.v. live your life like a motherfucker.

& this for

whatever reason made you trip over your own feet because you had

just been tested with your new baby in your belly & the nurse didn't

even act terrified when she accidentally poked herself with the needle she

just used on you

& you & your baby in your belly walk down the lepers' hallway

which also has signs in 10 other languages & you think those

signs say *this is the hallway for the risky lepers (welcome)*

& enter the clinic side for risky pregnant women & they tell

you since you are below the poverty line, unwed, black, under 21

no insurance, unprotected sex (just one time after church couldn't

hold it in any longer, pull out method) & std & hiv results inconclusive

in the system right now that you are high, high risk & that doctor enters the room with gloves on & you are already ass touching bottom

of table cold noodle legs wide archless feet in cuffs when he says

he's just gonna do a pelvic exam to see how pregnant you might

or might not be & it won't hurt so bad & plus *this must be your 2nd or 3rd*

baby & you tell him you don't handle pelvic exams very well & to please

go slow & he gets all burt reynolds & says *is that what you told your*

baby's daddy & you cannot be a smart ass because his whole hand

is (in)side you & you've got that baby in(side) too & this is when

you realize life is not about you (anymore) life is not about what

you want or what or wish or need or your favorite cookies or you (at all)

which is to say not again which is to say not ever

RE/[MEMBER]

you remember scoffing at math
all the adding negative numbers
& feeling incongruent (inside yourself)
how you wanted to tell your math teacher
you never understood what the purpose
was for _____
is it right to set a person up with so many
possibilities for failure/is it right to make
a person solve for x

you remember forgetting your
locker combination turning left
& right & sitting inside your center
how the people next to you did it so
easily as if they always had lockers
as if they were expert crackers
at codes at making any two digit
thing (work) magic

you remember feeling like you were magic
that you (yourself) were a code to be
cracked but instead you went for yolk

(v.) confession # 262
when no one watches
i moonwalk on my wooden floors
& do a little watch me now turn
because i miss michael jackson
& it doesn't matter anymore if he
had a big nose or a thin nose or...

TALK TO YOU IN THE MORNING

you know your hoodie is no cover or keep warm for your skin

(brown girl) you cannot even wear a berka for protection (sister)

if you traipse down the block naked even jesus the lord (himself)

would offer you a green leaf for your nakedness (woman with an

issue) be damned how you (woke) up next to your bodies self a

cradle of imperfections on an ebola kind of day (retch) yourself

spill every god particle & give it an atom mediocre meteor is

what they call you cloudy & no spark & how do you keep it

moving anyway (little girl) suffer yourself a fever of disbelief tell

your soul its not trapped but grounded (baby) feed the night

with empty calories weigh your grief in the mourning

BOOK OF MATTHEW (LEVI)

1.

& the storm rose up

2.

& the storm rose up higher

3.

& the heavens fell on earth which was so barren she could not hold the weight of
    heavens tears

4.

& the the floods they did come each wave licking & lapping (leapers) & we shall
    call you matthew

5.

& you will not be healed but heave

6.

& we will call the dead (dead)

7.

& the dead they are risen & hidden & no tree trunk is without a soul & no piece
    of soil is without a brain

8.

& no headlines or aid is fast enough

9.

amen/all men/ay man/hey man

(v.) psa from the ocean: when you gonna learn how to swim. learn how to separate sea shells from rocks. a splash from a wave. that ocean said listen girl, we ain't got all night to remind you of your worth. of your high priestess way & your magic. said you better dip yourself like the women before you. tell that fear & disappointment to find a sandcastle to destroy. you are not destined for stop drop & lay down & die. this is no time for why or what or how come. stop all your whine & bone & give thanks you've got a pot to piss in & a full tank of gas to get you home. tell your hands thank you for holding your heart. said how can you have the audacity to be sad when death is all around & motherfuckers are whaling on the inside like flesh sucking up a bag of forgotten bones. get yourself together. love don't live here anymore & you did not win the lottery & the people that committed the wrongs will not all the sudden get right. gone & dip yourself. see that magic do what it needs to do. tell that pity to find itself a new home. one with a baptismal pool & a clear space to pee.

THE NEW GUY

the new guy talks about his white woman like she is a prize
& a handshake & a spin the wheel & get 1,000 & we are not
angry that he blah blah blah's about his white woman like she is
everything we are not steam coming out of a bull's nostrils when
he says she is the most beautiful thing he's ever seen (no) we
only feel this & that way when he never calls his mother or sister
or daughter beautiful & when he never thinks anything brown
or tan is perfect or pure. the new guy is white (too) but he wears
his privilege like a black hoodie so as not to be found out (right
away) & he tells me one day in the break room you don't look
so bad for a black girl says to me with both hands in his gap jean
pockets *you kinda look as good as my girlfriend in that dress & i bet it
didn't take you hours to know what you want. white girls take all day
trying to decide but you…i bet you know what you want & you get it
(girl)* & you know in that moment he's trying to bleach you a
little trying to make you feel like you could be taylor swift or
miley cyrus or even monica lewinsky.

SAINTS

I.

saint of disgust & woe

holy ghost to this saint when
you feel fuckery across
the land when you just
can't
do
it (can't say can't in english)
any longer. when you
are at whoa whoa whoa
& die motherfucker

what she requires on her altar:

1 small turd
1 vial of tears (any persons will do)
1 lie you can't forget
1 truth you refuse to remember
1 apology you never received
1 white persons privilege
1 false promise/prophet/promotion
2 lumps of _____ (left) there

2.

& every tongue shall not confess

for this is the time of unraveled saints

& no bodies will wriggle

& no david praise dance will shake you

& no eyes rolling (this) & (that) way will whiten your black teeth

god is dead

(ass serious)

when she says she is in you &

& if she is in you then you must be

in you

 & if you are a vacant house of stagnant

do not expect a movement

THINGS I'VE HEARD PEOPLE TELL GIRLS AT TWELVE & GIRLS WHO WOKE UP ONE DAY WITH A PAIR OF BOOBS

you are not my little girl anymore

no more ice cream cones in public/don't order an ice cream cone anymore, from

now on get your ice cream in the cup/you cannot order vanilla ice cream

       anymore it doesn't look right on your lips.

you gonna be fast just like your mama/do you want to be fast/you must be one

       of those fast girls

no more jump rope, bike riding or tag for you find something less physical to do.

cover up/cover it up/cover them up/bind them/shove them/scoot them/

       pinch them

you will probably be pregnant by next year anyway

damn you look like you about 25   *you are not my little*

girl anymore

you gonna be fast just like your mama/do you want to be fast/you must be one

       of those fast girls

can't you find any jeans that don't show the shape of your behind/what do you

expect boys to do when you have jeans/genes like that/get a pair two sizes too

       big/i never looked like that at your age

you know you can get pregnant if you lust after a boy right/

don't hug your daddy anymore/don't hug your uncle anymore/ don't hug your

cousin anymore/ do not hug anymore.   *you are not my little*

girl anymore

you grown now/you're a grown woman now/how could someone with boobs

        that big still act like a 12-year-old?

use what you got to get what you want/shake what cha mama gave you/twerk it/

        work it/grind it/ride it

                    hide it

you gonna be fast just like your mama/do you want to be fast/you must be one

        of those fast girls

tampons are only for girls who have had sex…are you having sex?

the menstrual cycle is god's way of punishing women/now that you have your

thing you have to watch out for boys/the curse is the worse   *you are not*

my little girl anymore

awesome you've gotten your period, now once you graduate from college & find

a nice young man & get engaged & then get married you can give us two cute

        little grandchildren

sleep in your bra

stop trying to be sexy/get it girl you look sexy

you are not my little girl anymore

(v.) if a 12-year-old girl defaces your desk with hand drawn pictures of breast/boobs/titties/ta-ta's/ the girlz & a bicycle red x be slow to anger remember they muffle her lungs at home squish her poppin lips between too old & too young not enough & too much if a girl scribbles in pencil it's because she feels she wants to be erased take her memories & wrap them in toilet paper like so (like) (so) like…so don't chastise that girl the next day tell that girl you love her writing how that same pencil shades a kick ass poem in a disgruntled haze

SOUL POWER

the black souls line up like carmine book spines & bobby pins

all of them thirsting to climb into a nest of a tangled

braids all of them grasping desperately to thoughts   hanging there

who would ever want to be a black soul have yourself waiting to

be resurrected after each small death

whoa to the soul who feels his fingerprints have been left behind

whoa to the soul who feels her breath   shallow & insipid

TRAIN

when we arrive at the beach we long to be like seagulls all of our
take flight effortless and squawk squawk squawk when we arrive
at the beach we notice our bodies are covered that our moist
feet are the only signs of our beach bodies. and we aren't sure
who told us first that we had beach bodies or why it was a thing
to have a beach body but we had them. her body was of course
more beach-y than mine all her supple and san francisco curves
nothing like my iowa backyard but we are here ( ).

2.

this is about the time before we knew our bodies were kinda up
for sale before we knew an innocent tan line could make a man
want to fuck us behind the lemonade stand with a kaleidoscope
beach ball in hand. and neither of us got fucked because of your
tan lines but you know—bad things do happen to good people
and this is what happened here ( ).

3.

and you might be asking yourself what this story is about but i
want to tell you it isn't about anything. there is nothing, not to
tell because it is all washed away sandcastle and one dollar glasses.
we skipped school because everyone else skipped school and we
are not followers but today we are not leaders because when you
are straight a's and student government you deserve to say fuck
that good girl shit every once in a while. and we did that here ( ).

4.

it is true neither of us likes ice cream too much or sausages or
red vines but because there's a beach store which sells those
things plus orange crush soda we decide to buy all those things
and the guy notices our tan lines and offers to put lotion on one
of our backs and we don't really think that's weird because—
well—we are young and its hot and we have tan lines and only
one bottle of sunscreen and if we burn too hard one of our
parents will know we skipped school and went to the beach. for
this reason yes is what fish jumps from the from the bridge of
our lips and we said this in unison as if we are not dry humping
girl friends but twins and he asked us after he scratched his
nose if were twins and he laughed the kind of laugh a rail road
conductor laughs and you might be asking what kind of laugh
that is and i will ask you if you've ever ridden a train.

VANISHING HITCHHIKER

I.

you are an urban myth: tooth fairy, boogieman, goblin, bloody mary—less real
than any argopelter.

the legend says you are an ascetic _____ holding the power of _____ & when
you beheld the eyes of your firstborn, you instantly became a pure bright light. of
course, the legend cannot be true. your daughter is a hangover.

can i be *your* american flag, not a girl left standing at the foot of a steel slide.

2.   VISIT 1

when you inhale pall mall like a white hollywood producer's pimp
i know you are dying. i hear them talk about you awkwardly like open thighs at
the obgyn. i hear them say your name in a lullaby hush. *father.*

VISIT 2

i search for the rumor of your smokey robinson eyes in my
smokey robinson eyes. you gulp— then ask, why i don't drink?
remember daddy: sepia album. always smiling cool. always drink in one hand.
always holding me in the other. always the bouquet of aramis armpit, domino
company & royal velvet bags hidden beneath honorably discharged mustang seats.
when they say shake it baby, i do.

VISIT 3

cadence. how it spins on my tongue like a fuzzy vinyl record. you are a powdery &
paralyzed purple haze. bus stopping. right. left.
rub your chin to keep from discussing disney land-life, enabling wife, two
stepdaughters & saxophone players riffing at leimert park.
you natter in a head nod. we speak in number two pencil.

VISIT 4

recognize the innards of notes, of moans, of atterly on yellow days.
you are open to discussing food. how to eat catfish bone in, tongue to the left,
only your mother's seasonings. okra & corn. creole & haitian. tell me through the
bathroom wall i was born blessedly cursed. you knew it when you sipped cognac
at the bar. your baby was a priestess. white robes & a bald head. I never knew you
were a leper/you never said you wanted healing/I always knew I should cut the
devil some s(lack).

VISIT 5

you reject the new crisp linen. what's the point?
when i found out you were born in october,
i ask jeeves: can libras be good fathers.

VISITATION

white candle flicker.

an abandoned poem. fathered.

broken glass.

talking tree.

trunk kisses. your sunken cheeks.

the smell of dead daddy & rejection

like sticky rice & plasma/like cemetery & coffee.

(v.) confession # 255
i wanted captain kangaroo to be my daddy
his happiness falling out of the television
like sun in seattle
like the super friends on the bad guys
like kindergarten pee after a tickle
& i didn't care that he was white & i was not
if he could love mr. green jeans, bunny rabbit & a moose
surely he'd love me.

3.

… was a good father to his three stepchildren & wife.
according to all of the neighborhood his heart was open
& he always helped out as many people as he could.
… was a vietnam veteran who earned two purple
hearts saving his whole platoon.

when asked from the casket
how you felt about your daughter you replied (who)

(v.) confession # 256
i wanted mr. rogers to be my daddy—too.
not because of his sweater
or his artistic abilities or his puppet skills
but because he was gentle
& what a daughter needs is a gentle dad
because even when your 7
the world is scheming on how to smack your ass
or how to fit you in a thong or a song.

ZOMBIE (2)

you hear that zombie sex has a peculiar smell like rotten egg plant
& placenta you hear that after it's over you will remember about
deep breaths about smiling &

          gyrating

you hear through honey covered maggots that it will make you feel
the way you used to feel when you were in neon & not in black & white
you hear you will unravel in a good way & anything that rips will be good

you hear that when you were a sort of lotus flower that your sex
was on fire that it was quiver & goddamn but you are a zombie (now)
& this cocktail of words does not go down/these words do not belong

          in your shuffle

you say in your zombie voice *what is quiver/what is smile/what is*

          faster—please

(v.) what is it like to surrender? is there a prologue with final instructions on how not to be?
does our strength grow wild in purgatory—is this why we always straddle the middle? we are
not interested in walking straight or being pointed or knives & spoons. we know the difference
between getting fucked & being forked.

CRUCIFIXES & CUM

I.

my pussy chants for amnesia but someone inside me remembers
these labia walls a place of prayer, that day a holy ghost on my lips.

2.

there are days when my clitoris doubles as a circus, the push & pull
juggling at the mercy of a little girl smelling of cotton candy. the sexy
gymnast wide legs & glitter.

3.

my fingers are an atlas at the mercy of ask about what happened & then…
a place of prayer, these labia walls, on my lips more holy than any ghost.

4.

someone inside me remembers an abandoned church with a backdoor & a
black jesus playing dominoes. these bones still slap. this place of prayer
more holy than any ghost. legs & glitter.

SKIPPER

MALIBU SKIPPER (BENDABLE LEGS) 1969-1983

SKIPPER (I)

me: how do you feel

skipper: how do you think i feel

skipper smelled like a combination of pickle juice & pussy
(which i liked) when she arrived she snatched her glasses off
& big girl tender'd to the right (*he's cute*) she puffed out
like a kid sister or baby dragon when she ordered bourbon
with a squeeze of lime i knew we would shit talk about barbie
as if she was still alive like she would glide down the
escalator in pink stilettos, stethoscope & stiff neck
(i think we both looked away at the same time)   then
skipper said something like *fuck barbie* her lips puckered
magenta as if she herself were made of plastic & ken   she said
sold the pink camper which skipper thought was selfish
because that's the place they fucked in the most—& i asked her
one final time if she was sure   she didn't love me
to which she replied *no bitch you are just too real* & we ate
our fries & dipped them in spam which was barbies favorite
spread & skipper (i decided) was never gonna grow up was never
gonna stop wearing that goddamned jumpsuit (the one i loved)

so skipper says to me in a low voice & loud hands that barbie's been drinking a lot lately & taking pills & i say to skipper what kind of pills & skipper says to me the kind of pills no one should take & this makes me angry because skipper is always vague & cryptic & no one who is so smart should be allowed to be saying things that sound like garble garble blank blank blank & she notices i have a what in the entire fuck look on my face & she says to me all tender & 70's brady bunch glow— maybe you should talk to barbie & i say i don't want to talk to barbie & anyway what does ken say about this & skipper tells me while unbuttoning my blouse that ken & barbie aren't really together together & when skipper moves herself closer to me i want to tell her she is beautiful. i want to tell her she doesn't have to keep being a sidekick or a kickstand & she says to me she's got no problem being second best that little girls secretly like her better (anyway) & then she says to me in what seems like slow motion   even   ken   does (too) there was a starry night i remember where the bits & pieces are all scrambled egg & hair tangly where skipper, barbie, ken & were intoxicated with summer & beer & wine & skipper said something like *ken you are such a boy* & barbie said (not really) & skipper & ken or maybe it was skipper & i or maybe it was ken & barbie—some of the pairs knew something or maybe one thing the other(s) did not (know). & that same night i combed barbies hair profusely because i was having company & wanted her to look just the part for the friend who was also bringing some doll i didn't care to not know. & skipper fell upon her bendable knees & said something like *i don't really care you can put my hair in a messy bun or not even comb it* (at all) & this is how the hearts were drawn/out of apathy out of the fact that she didn't give a flying fuscia fuck about her hair or shoes or crooked lip (stick) & she wasn't all oh oh me me me look at me don't you want me about herself. & ken & i took a step outside by the camper & toasted to a woman who didn't need our validation or any hu(man) to bring her to her knees.

& scene

scene i.

(top)

in the days when we made love every day we held the window open with our bottle of soy sauce because we never used it unless we ate sushi which we rarely did because she didn't like it & today while waiting for her to cum i realize that our soy sauce bottle isn't full anymore, that there's small soy sauce crusties on the left side where smooth red top used to be, that she's not calling me daddy or baby or fuck me harder & this makes me feel raw & slimy like

scene i.

(bottom)

in the days when we made love everyday we held the window open with our bottle of soy sauce because we never used it unless we ate sushi which we never did because i don't like it because it makes me turn my face up like a little suburban kid forced to eat brussels sprouts the day before the 4th of july. i can't seem to cum because i know that bottle of soy sauce is going to say what i want to say—that something is going on & i've been slathering avocados with it. that i've been licking the rim the way i lick her nipples carefully & circle circle circle. that i once tongued the red tops bottom in an effort to get it all & i can't manage to call her daddy or baby or fuck me harder because all i really want is more salt in my wounds. something anything to make this ouch fade away.

scene ii.
(top to bottom)

why didn't you cum
why is the soy sauce down to the label?
why won't you look at me
what did i do

scene ii.
(bottom to top)

i don't know (this is a truth)
i don't know (this is a lie)
i don't know (this is a truth)
i don't know (this is a lie)

when skipper told me that she was adopted i admit that i didn't think it was a big deal—i know a lot of people who are adopted & when she told me she had some hard times growing up i didn't flinch or have any pity for her & when she told me about the time her adopted parents left her home alone for a whole weekend & she ate a lot mayonnaise sandwiches, ritz spreadable cheese on white bread butts & slippery sardines from the can i still wasn't feeling nearly as boo-hoo or cry me a river as maybe some people would. skipper was nipple hard & so was i but when she sang that damn song quote *papa was a rolling stone wherever he laid his hat was his home* for whatever reason i could feel the tears start to form the way ice acts like it wants to take over a refrigerated glass & she said what she meant to say was after she was adopted her father fathered at least 4 (more) kids & i said what do you mean (more) since you were adopted & then she said well my dad actually got another woman pregnant & then he & his wife adopted me & i said so your father is your biological father & she said yes & his oldest daughter is my biological mother & i couldn't help but puke out the pepsi i was drinking from the hot can & she said nope not all kids born of siblings are _____ & i said with a kind of forrest gump smirk i think you are beautiful & she said ken was right, he told me you had a hard time seeing & that you needed glasses.

a bor tion.

a bor tion.

a bor tion.

on the last round of drinks skipper made us say it three times each. she said she liked
the way barbie said it better said she was going for the voice of judgment or lament
or quaker girl like her mother or you should know better kind of tone (which was
perfect for barbie) & barbie didn't find this *sort of thing* funny at all—in fact skipper
& i watched like calico cats as barbies panties began to ruffle right before our eyes
& we were both looking at her panties ruffle because we had each had maybe 6
drinks a piece & barbie sat with her legs open as if she was gonna pee right there in
the pink posh bar (the actual name) & then i said to skipper i think barbies gonna
pee her panties & her panties made a crunching sound like crushed leaves/crushed
almonds/crushed hearts/ **a bor tion** barbie said is *not the right answer skipper* to
which skipper replied are you adding preacher to your list of jobs & this is when
it happened barbie's head fell right off in front of us/first swivel/then backwards/
then fall. & skipper asked me to put it back on this time said she was tired of always
putting her perfection back together again

you wear a canary raincoat
as if you are afraid to get wet
as if you have never sat shivering   in (the) cold
as if your hands have never been   slippery

& this is when i show you there
is a hole in your sleeve where
you keep the secrets & you
realize there are droplets skipping
on your shoulders   in the cold
                                                      s(lip)pery

SUBSTITUTION

& your name shall be jazz.

sold. to the highest bidder.

smooth proprietary pimps.

make you holler kenny g & krall

forge your name in curly fonts

stick you between corporate happy hours & red wine

un-riff roots

show—just enough to present you exotically acceptable

a hint of kink—an etta james remake

from a single lady—

vegetarians speaking byrd. suburban babies named coltrane.

no brown in sight for miles & miles

davis & nina simone. sold.

public radio tries to resurrect who you is/was.

sold. to the highest bidder.

bebop only when there is bbq chicken. watermelon. poverty.

just be in the blackground against broad daylight.

(v.) blanche calloway,
horace silver,
sarah vaughan,
dexter gordon,
dinah washington,
wc handy,
maxine sullivan,
lee morgan,
nancy wilson,
louis armstrong,
nina simone,
king oliver,
haxzel scott,
carmen mcray,
eubie blake,

alice coltrane,
charles mingus,
mary lou williams,
dizzy gillespie,
etta jones,
thelonious monk,
etta james,
miles davis,
billie holiday,
kid ory,
lena horn,
art blakey,
bessie smith,
john coltrane,
melba liston,
sidney bechet,
alberta hunter,
marian mc portland,
coleman hawkins,
duke ellington,
sun ra,
shirley horn,
max roach,
lil hardin armstrong,
mildred bailey,
cannonball adderley,
earnestine anderson,
nat king cole,
esther phillips,
betty carter,
cab calloway

AFTERWORD

REZINA HABTEMARIAM

To be Black in this country is to have an intimate relationship with premature death as a result of state perpetrated and sanctioned violence. To be a Black woman in this country is to have our bodies animalized, marked by a legacy of both racialized and gendered violence. It would take college courses in Black literature (always electives), Black feminist texts, and communities of Black women to help me process, gain the language, and analysis to connect hypervisible assaults to the racialized and gendered aggressions I experienced on the playground and in the classroom and at the dance and in the grocery store and at the mall and at the party and, and, and. Which is to say, I did not fully understand and could not deftly articulate the relationship between the identities I embody and the systemic oppression(s) that characterized everyday life until adulthood.

(v.) is Anastacia-Reneé's necessary intervention to disrupt this paradigm. This stunning collection is a raw meditation on the politics brutally imposed on the bodies of Black girls and women. Through critical poetics, Renee maps the violent conditions that shape the material realities of our lives and in doing so, provides a compass that helps us navigate and (re)claim power. *(v.)* explores how realities of hypersexualization, erasure, denial of adolescence/womanhood/humanity informs how we move through this world. Reneé interrogates what she poignantly describes as small deaths and the fracturing of selves they cause. In this way, *(v.)* serves as

a cautionary tale for Black girls of when: you are stopped by the police, you are told that you are too dark and your lips too big, benediction is given daily for Black lives taken, you birth babies that become targets that tell you "they're trying to kill us mama", your sexuality is spectacle, your culture is colonized, your body is stolen and you wonder if it was ever even yours.

(v.) is an assemblage of the lessons painfully realized and learned from the violence of daily life. It is an archive of knowledge grounded in the collective experiences of Black women who have always made a way out of no(way). I wonder what it would have meant to have access to this subjugated knowledge earlier in life. If I'd known then that part of what it means to be a Black girl (and woman) in this country is to be systematically positioned at the bottom, how would I have internalized the socio-historical constructed boundaries of my personhood differently? Perhaps in centering Black cultural and knowledge production earlier, I would have cultivated a practice of self-definition sooner. Perhaps in learning to expect the small deaths, I would have been less disappointed, better able to recover, and keep it movin'…

Anastacia-Reneé's scripture is two middle fingers up to a world that does not want to see a Black girl flying. *(v.)* is affirmation of our worth and the interconnectedness of our survival. It is reminder that we are here because of holy lineages of Black women who imagined freedom. Renee urges us to continue radical Black feminist tradition and bare witness to our (her) stories, testify our truth, and demand our collective liberation.

A C K N O W L E D G M E N T S

give thanks to dead writers, activist & dreamers who came
before me—who guide me when writing feels isolating,
lackluster & barren. give thanks to framily (friends & family)
who support & honor my writing & welcome my consistent
alien-like creativity. give thanks to every writer in my inner-
circle who took a look at *(v.)* & gave me relentless & honest
feedback (some more than once!). give thanks to everyone
who invested in the belief, concept & environment of *(v.)*
from start to finish. give thanks to my partner naa akua for
unconditional love & ginger beer'd insomnia re(vision)
nights. cheers.

ANASTACIA-RENEÉ IS THE WRITER-IN-RESIDENCE AT HUGO HOUSE, WORKSHOP FACILITATOR AND MULTIVALENT PERFORMANCE ARTIST. ALONG WITH *(V.)*, HER BOOKS *FORGET IT* (BLACK RADISH BOOKS) AND *ANSWER(ME)* (WINGED CITY CHAPBOOKS-ARGUS PRESS) WILL BE PUBLISHED IN 2017.